XTREME SURVIVAL

SURVIVING THE RAINFOREST

A&D Xtreme
BOLD HI-LO NONFICTION
An imprint of Abdo Publishing
abdobooks.com

JESSICA RUSICK

TAKE IT TO THE XTREME!

GET READY FOR AN EXTREME ADVENTURE! THE PAGES OF THIS BOOK WILL TAKE YOU INTO THE THRILLING WORLD OF OUTDOOR SURVIVAL. WHEN YOU HAVE FINISHED READING THIS BOOK, TAKE THE XTREME CHALLENGE ON PAGE 45 ABOUT WHAT YOU'VE LEARNED!

ABDOBOOKS.COM
Published by Abdo Publishing, a division of ABDO, PO Box 398166, Minneapolis, Minnesota 55439.

Printed in the United States of America, North Mankato, MN.
102023
012024

THIS BOOK CONTAINS RECYCLED MATERIALS

Design: Tamara JM Peterson, Mighty Media, Inc.
Editor: Katherine Chu
Cover Photographs: high fliers/Shutterstock Images (rainforest); mara86pred/Shutterstock Images (tiger)
Interior Photographs: Al'fred/Shutterstock Images, pp. 4–5; Ammit Jack/Shutterstock Images, pp. 34–35; AP Images, pp. 10–11; Archedmaid/Wikimedia Commons, p. 27; banjongseal168/Shutterstock Images, pp. 22–23; BorneoRimbawan/Shutterstock Images, pp. 32–33; Cocos.Bounty/Shutterstock Images, pp. 8–9; Gigoliver/Shutterstock Images, pp. 26–27; high fliers/Shutterstock Images, p. 1 (rainforest); Juriah Mosin/Shutterstock Images, pp. 14–15; Laurence/Adobe Stock, pp. 18–19; M Stocker/Shutterstock Images, pp. 12–13; mara86pred/Shutterstock Images, p. 1 (tiger); Maria Koepcke/Hans-Wilhelm Koepcke/Wikimedia Commons, p. 4; Maridav/Shutterstock Images, pp. 16–17; Mark Green/Shutterstock Images, pp. 38–39; mortenrochssare/Shutterstock Images, pp. 28–29; Pedro Helder Pinheiro/Shutterstock Images, p. 46; Robert/Adobe Stock, pp. 20–21; SL-Photography/Shutterstock Images, pp. 24–25; studiomiracle/Shutterstock Images, pp. 30–31; Teo Tarras/Shutterstock Images, p. 44; Vaclav Sebek/Shutterstock Images, pp. 40–43; Vladimir Wrangel/Shutterstock Images, pp. 36–37; worldclassphoto/Shutterstock Images, pp. 6–7
Design Elements: Nik Merkulov/Shutterstock Images (grunge background); queezz/Shutterstock Images (brush texture)

Library of Congress Control Number: 2023939332

Publisher's Cataloging-in-Publication Data
Names: Rusick, Jessica, author.
Title: Surviving the rainforest / by Jessica Rusick
Description: Minneapolis, Minnesota : Abdo Publishing, 2024 | Series: Xtreme survival | Includes online resources and index.
Identifiers: ISBN 9781098291853 (lib. bdg.) | ISBN 9781098278755 (ebook)
Subjects: LCSH: Survival--Juvenile literature. | Survival skills--Juvenile literature. | Forests and forestry--Accidents--Juvenile literature. | Jungle survival--Juvenile literature. | Outdoor life--Juvenile literature. | Wilderness survival--Juvenile literature.
Classification: DDC 613.69--dc23

TABLE OF CONTENTS

CHAPTER 1

THE CRASH

When Koepcke was 14, her family founded the Panguana research station in the Amazon. Koepcke lived there for two years before moving back to Lima to finish high school.

On December 24, 1971, teenager Juliane Koepcke boarded a flight in Lima, Peru. She was traveling to her parents' **research** station in the Amazon rainforest. But halfway into the flight, lightning struck the plane. It broke apart in midair, falling thousands of feet into the rainforest below.

Koepcke fell about 10,000 feet (3,000 m) during the crash. Her injuries included a broken collarbone, a deep cut on her arm, and a swollen eye.

Koepcke awoke alone on the rainforest floor. Luckily, she survived the fall with only moderate injuries. Koepcke's parents had taught her what to do if she ever became lost in the rainforest. Now she would put that teaching into practice. How would she survive?

The rainforest is a **dangerous** place to become **stranded**. The thick growth is difficult to walk through. **Venomous** snakes, fierce jaguars, and **disease**-carrying mosquitoes are constant **threats**. But Koepcke and many others have overcome these dangers and more, thanks to their survival skills.

XTREME FACT

There are rainforests on every continent except Antarctica. The Amazon rainforest is the largest, covering nearly 40 percent of South America.

To avoid the thick growth, Koepcke swam in the middle of the river. She kept an eye out for stingrays near the riverbanks and piranhas in the river.

SURVIVOR SPOTLIGHT

Koepcke found a nearby stream to drink from to stay hydrated. She followed the stream, which became a river. She knew that humans usually settle along rivers and hoped she would find someone to help her. After ten days, Koepcke found a small shack. The shack's owners found her the next day, and she was rescued!

Koepcke knew many rainforest plants and animals are toxic to humans. So she avoided eating things she did not recognize.

CHAPTER 2

FINDING WATER

If possible, purify any water you find by boiling it or using purification tablets.

Finding water is the most important part of any survival situation. Without water, people become dehydrated. Dehydration is when the body loses water. It can cause confusion, weakness, and eventually death. Because the rainforest is hot and humid, it can cause people to sweat, making the body lose water quicker. So it's important to stay hydrated.

XTREME FACT

Humans can only survive for about three days without water.

Luckily, rainforests are full of water. Some rainforests receive hundreds of inches of rain per year! Rainwater is the safest water source in an emergency. In 2023, Jhonattan Acosta became lost in the rainforest while hunting. To survive, he used his boots to collect rainwater!

Acosta was rescued after spending 31 days in the Amazon rainforest.

There are different ways to get drinking water in the rainforest. Bamboo and vines can be sources of water. Make a cut at a bamboo stalk joint or cut away a section of vine. Water may drain out! Rivers are another water source. But they contain parasites that can make people sick, so avoid drinking from them if possible.

Water bottles, shoes, and large leaves can all hold or catch water from rain, bamboo, or vines.

CHAPTER 3
STAYING DRY

The rainforest's constant dampness can take a **toll** on the body. One way to keep dry is to build a shelter. In 2021, pilot Antonio Sena's plane crashed in the Amazon. As he **navigated** the rainforest, Sena built shelters on high ground, away from sources of water to avoid flooding. He also covered the shelters with palm fronds.

XTREME FACT

Being in wet rainforests often causes foot fungus infections. Fungus thrives in warm, wet conditions, such as those in a shoe.

Sena traveled during the mornings. He found a safe spot to build a shelter in the early afternoons. He built his shelter and fire in the late afternoons.

There are many different types of shelters. One simple shelter is a lean-to. It's made by leaning a large branch against a tree. Smaller branches lean against the big branch and are covered in leaves and other greenery.

A lean-to is the easiest shelter to make. It only requires branches and greenery.

A fire can be used to cook food and repel mosquitoes. It may also frighten away larger predators.

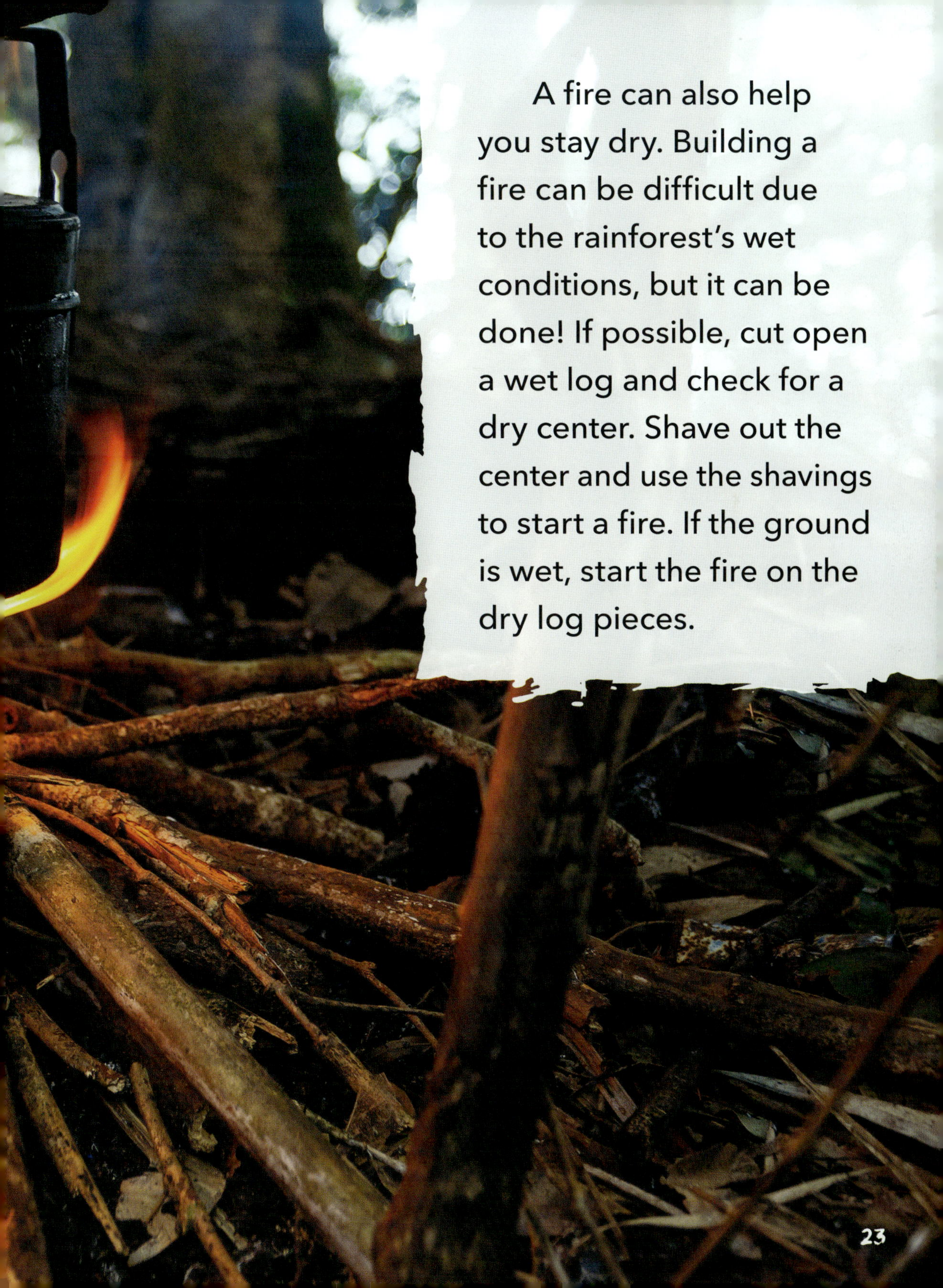

A fire can also help you stay dry. Building a fire can be difficult due to the rainforest's wet conditions, but it can be done! If possible, cut open a wet log and check for a dry center. Shave out the center and use the shavings to start a fire. If the ground is wet, start the fire on the dry log pieces.

CHAPTER 4

FINDING FOOD

There are many fruits, nuts, and plants to forage for in the rainforest. Some are safe to eat. But others are poisonous. Avoid eating anything you don't recognize. Look for familiar food sources, such as coconuts, citrus fruits, and peanuts.

XTREME FACT

Castor bean is a dangerous rainforest plant. It contains ricin, a poisonous substance. Even a small amount of ricin can kill someone in days.

Sena observed the fruit that monkeys ate. This showed Sena which fruit was safe for him too!

Be resourceful when finding food. Acosta ate worms and other insects. Another survivor, Yossi Ghinsberg, ate berries and eggs from abandoned birds' nests.

Ghinsberg was lost in the Amazon rainforest for three weeks in 1981.

If you catch fish, don't save any leftovers, as they can attract other wildlife. Fish will also spoil quickly due to the rainforest's heat and humidity.

Hunting for food is often not worth the time and energy. It's better to think about finding water and shelter. It's also easy to get injured while chasing prey. Still, there are several ways to hunt. One is to sharpen a bamboo stalk or stick to spear fish. Traps made with sticks and large rocks can also catch and crush small animals.

CHAPTER 5

NAVIGATING SAFELY

It's difficult to walk through the rainforest. Plants, vines, fallen tree trunks, and other **obstacles** make it easy to become lost. To avoid confusion, try walking in one direction. Look for landmarks or mark your path to make sure you are not traveling in circles. Walk during the day when it's easiest to see.

Leave a trail to avoid walking in circles. Mark trees with torn clothing or any bright objects you find.

Sena established a daily plan to **navigate** the rainforest. In the morning, he would walk in one direction, using the sun to stay on course. He would set up camp in the afternoon and sleep at night. Sena's survival skills paid off. After 36 days, he encountered workers in the rainforest and was rescued!

Sena was rescued 17 miles (27 km) from where his plane crashed.

Sena used a pocketknife to cut through vines and branches.

Another way to **navigate** the rainforest is to look for animal trails while walking. They may lead to open spaces or water. Find a large stick to push plants, vines, and other **obstacles** out of the way. Avoid touching things with your hands. You could get bitten, poked, or stung!

CHAPTER 6

ANIMAL ENCOUNTERS

The rainforest is full of **dangerous** animals. Anacondas and stingrays live near riverbanks. Mosquitoes are also a **threat**. Their bites cause itching and pain, and they can carry **diseases** that make humans sick. Cover exposed skin with cloth or mud to prevent mosquito bites.

Green anacondas live in the Amazon. They do not normally eat humans unless they are very hungry. But it's best to avoid them just in case.

Jaguars also live in the rainforest. To avoid a jaguar attack, it's important to stand your ground. Back away slowly and try to scare the jaguar by raising your arms. Or get resourceful! Ghinsberg encountered a jaguar when he was **stranded**. He used a lighter to set fire to a spray of mosquito repellent, scaring the jaguar away!

XTREME FACT

Jaguars usually don't attack humans unless they are startled or provoked.

If you see a jaguar, never turn your back or run away.

CHAPTER 7

GETTING RESCUED

Rescuers sometimes use airplanes to look for people **stranded** in the rainforest. If you are in an airplane crash, stay near the wreckage for as long as possible. It's easier for rescuers to spot wreckage from the air. Try to hail passing aircraft by burning damp leaves to make thick smoke.

Try to find an open area with less tree cover. Waving a reflective object can catch the attention of passing rescue planes.

Unfortunately, thick tree cover often makes it hard for rescuers to spot people. In many cases, the only way to get rescued is to find other people. Following a river, like Koepcke did, is the best way to do this. Look and listen for signs that humans are nearby. Sena was rescued after following the sound of a chainsaw!

Koepcke could identify different bird calls. When she heard the call of a hoatzin, a bird that lives near open areas of water, she knew there may be people nearby.

XTREME FACT

Survival experts say one of the most important survival skills is staying calm. Thinking clearly helps people survive!

CHAPTER 8

SURVIVING THE RAINFOREST

Being **stranded** in the rainforest means having little **access** to shelter, food, and dry conditions. **Dangerous** animals are constant **threats**. But with top-notch survival skills and a bit of luck, some people have overcome these challenges to survive. Think back on the rainforest survival stories you read and skills you learned. Could you survive in the rainforest?

To survive, don't take unnecessary risks or do anything dangerous. Find ways to safely navigate the rainforest and avoid injuries.

XTREME CHALLENGE

TAKE THE QUIZ BELOW AND PUT WHAT YOU'VE LEARNED TO THE TEST!

1) What did Juliane Koepcke follow when she was looking for civilization?

2) How do you build a lean-to shelter?

3) What did Jhonattan Acosta use to catch rainwater?

4) How can you protect yourself from mosquito bites?

5) How would you stay calm if you were stranded in the rainforest?

GLOSSARY

access–the opportunity to gain or use something.

dangerous–able or likely to cause hurt or harm.

disease–a sickness.

expert–a person very knowledgeable about a certain subject.

fungus–an organism, such as mold or mildew, that grows on organic matter.

infection–a disease caused by the presence of bacteria or other germs.

navigate–to find the way from place to place.

obstacle–something that you have to go over or around.

provoke—to cause a person or animal to become angry or violent.

research—the study of something to learn new information.

stranded—lacking the means to leave a place.

threat—something that could be harmful.

toll—a cost in life or health.

venomous—producing poison.

ONLINE RESOURCES

To learn more about rainforest survival, please visit **abdobooklinks.com** or scan this QR code. These links are routinely monitored and updated to provide the most current information available.

INDEX